THE KINGDOM COME

Written and Illustrated by Carol Erickson

I dedicate this book to the hearts and minds of those who read it. May you find new significance to your own lives and the reasons for which you were born.

I express appreciation to Jess, his little sister Katie, Jenny, my husband, son, daughter-in-law and grandchildren for being my models.

A special thanks to my children who helped with this project, and Doug Jordan, my airbrush instructor, who made me believe in myself.

© 1994 Carol Erickson
The Kingdom Come
All rights reserved
Second Printing
Library of Congress # 93-85997
ISBN # 1-55517-145-1
Printed in the United States of America

Dwelling in the Heavens above
        is a kind, gentle Father
        filled with love.

He watches over all the earth
        and tenderly guides you
        from the time of your birth.

He knows all your thoughts
        and wherever you roam,
        His spirit can touch you
        from this heavenly home.

Heaven is splendid
    like a glorious morn;
    it is where we all lived
    before we were born.

The spirits who live there
    have peace of mind;
    and just like our Father
    are loving and kind.

There are angels who bring you
    clean laundry each day,
    and angels who sweep
    all the moondust away.

Everyone's helpful, generous and true;
    but somehow I feel
    I need something new.

Everywhere are children
so cheery and sweet;
it's laughter and playtime
whenever they meet.

Then up with the dawn
through the heavens they run,
gathering dewdrops
in the rays of the sun.

Sometimes the children
can even be seen
using the clouds
as a trampoline.

The children are joyful, but I must confess,
    I'm not happy—my name is Jess.
I feel a longing and I don't know why;
    sometimes I even want to cry.

There's Katie, Billy, Jenny and June
    dancing around in the light of the moon.
With the fun that we have and the things that we do,
    I can't understand why I still feel blue.

One day I was bored, but said with a grin,
  I'll play a game of tag with the wind.
But I grew tired before I was done,
  and sat down to think in the rays of the sun.

I wonder what's wrong with me—why am I bored?
  I must have a problem . . .
      I'll go talk with the Lord.

He listened intently and with soft-spoken eyes,
said, "I understand, Son."
He is so wise!

In the palm of his hands He held my face,
I was in awe of his glorious grace.
I knew full well this wondrous Man
could control the earth with one command.
Yet in His presence, inside I could feel
an inner peace that was very real.

He slowly walked over and calm as could be,
    said, "Bring all the children unto me."
We knelt at His feet and sat quietly;
    though everyone listened—He was talking to ME!

There are many things you don't understand;
    it's time you know I have a plan.
Here in the Heavens things run so smooth,
    you haven't a chance your character to prove.
A body you'll need to be tested and tried,
    with temptation on earth from every side.

Earth life has beauty, sorrow and pain;
    it is all the experience you need to gain.
Without these trials, the thing that I fear,
    you'll never appreciate what you have here.
You must feel sorrow to recognize joy;
    otherwise, you'll be an ungrateful boy.

While on the earth you'll learn to care
    for the people who have heavy burdens to bear.
The suffering you see as you cling to the rod
    may make you doubt the existence of GOD.

It's a test, don't you see, and one I must send;
    for the way that you meet it counts in the end.
I cannot tell you what sorrow you'll know;
    that's a chance you must take if you still want to go.

There is one thing that you must be aware;
    the forces of SATAN are everywhere.
He will tempt you with pleasure, fun and games,
    but all he will bring you is sorrow and pain.

Between good and evil you must learn to choose;
    free agency will be yours to use.
But, just before you make your choice,
    listen for the whisperings of my voice;
    and deep within your heart you'll know
    right from wrong—which way to go.

Your earthly family will always be near;
    they'll guide and protect, so you needn't fear.
You must be strong, you must resist,
    I'll always be with you if you persist.

Keep the commandments, your parents obey;
    and above all . . . remember to pray.
If you prove yourselves worthy and return to me,
    together we'll dwell in eternity.

Soon it will be time to choose one of you
  to go down to earth, and carry my plan through.
The angel will come with a name on a scroll;
  announcing the time for someone to go.

I jumped to my feet, for suddenly I knew,
　　this was just the thing I wanted to do!

I said, "Father, please, can I be the one
　　to explore PLANET EARTH and make sure things are done?
I'll be an example—a guiding light!
　　just give me a MOTHER—I'm ready tonight!"

God said, "My Son,

All mothers are pretty, all mothers are fun,
    but we must select a special one.
One clean and holy, and righteous, you see?
    To show you the light so you'll come back to me."

We searched the world over—looked far and wide,
    He spoke many things as I walked by His side.
Let's look for a mother gentle and mild,
    ready to give of herself for a child.

All at once, we found her and somehow I knew . . .
    as a beautiful MOTHER came into view.
Praying for a baby, waiting patiently,
    for one so sweet and lovely . . .
                JUST LIKE ME!

And right there beside her loving and true,
    was a big, handsome DAD who wanted me too!

This mother has eaten all the right foods,
    and promised she'll be in kind, loving moods.
Although you'll have problems from day to day,
    together with a father, they'll show you the way.

I've made WOMAN my partner and we act as one . . .
    to bring forth my children in worlds to come.

I could not wait—I thought I'd burst
        with happiness inside.
I turned so many somersaults,
        my feet began to glide.
I'll hurry fast and pack my things
        and be so clean and tidy;
It made me laugh when Father said,
        "You don't even need a nightie."

So the seed of life was planted deep
within my mother's womb.
And in time, just like a flower,
my body would blossom and bloom.

With scroll in hand, the Angel came,
and loud and clear she called MY NAME!!

As I turned to my friends, I could see
    through tears of joy they were happy for me.
With tender thoughts of the love we share,
    I found it hard to leave them there.
But, little Katie, my special friend,
    I felt somehow I would see again.

At that moment I knew my choice was not wrong,
    for the Heavenly Angels burst into song.
The time had come to leave His side,
    I hugged Him tenderly;
    but as we said our last goodbye,
    He spoke these words to me:

"Remember Son, while on the earth to spread my word to man,
    and take the simple message of my loving gospel plan."

"I will, I promise, Father; I'll report to you each day
    and ask you for your guidance so I'll never go astray.
I'll keep all the commandments, you'll be so proud of me.
    I'll be good, so very good . . . as good as good can be!"

Then all at once I knew the time had come to go,
    I slid down a moonbeam to the EARTH below.

"I WANT TO HAVE A BABY," my MOM does insist;
   she doesn't even know that already I EXIST!

I might be just a tiny dot, too small for eyes to see,
   but already it's determined exactly what I'll be.

My eyes are brown, my hair is blonde,
   of course, a BOY I'll be.
What I'm really trying to tell you is,
   already I AM ME!

At ten days old, if you could see,
    an Embryo is what I'd be.
My goodness, how alarming!
    I'm not sure that this is ME!

My mouth is beginning to open now,
    and I am remembering so,
    the way I laughed in Heaven
    just eighteen days ago.

My heart began to beat today
    and I can surely tell,
    though I am only three weeks old
    I am ALIVE AND WELL.

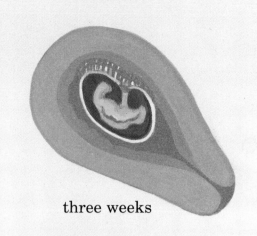

three weeks

At one month old, my arms and legs
    are beginning to form.
And I am dreaming dreams of
    what they will perform.
I will climb the highest mountain,
    operate a big machine.
Hug my Daddy, pet a puppy,
    go wading in a stream.

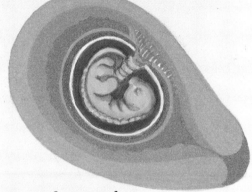

four weeks

At five weeks old I have fingers
    and toes, just look at me!
Will I play the piano,
    or will I plant a tree?

My Mother isn't feeling well,
    she thinks she has the flu.
Dad took her to the Doctor
    to see what he could do.
He checked her over thoroughly,
    as careful as could be,
    and then he smiled warmly
    . . . and told her IT WAS ME.

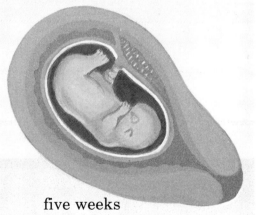

five weeks

At nine weeks old my face is formed,
    my eyes are able to see.
It's dark all around, but I'm not afraid
    . . . MOMMY is caring for me.

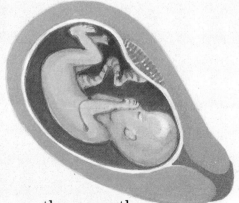

three months

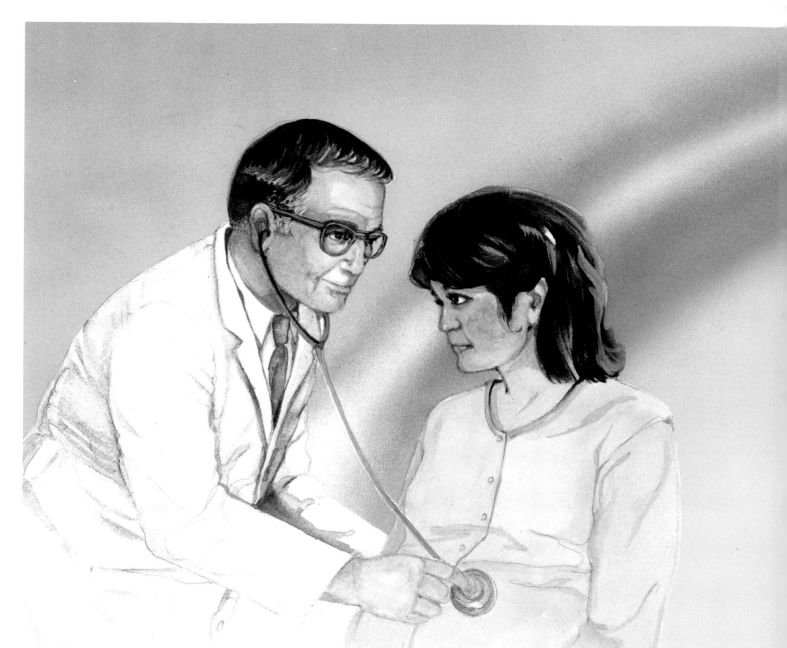

My parents are so happy with feelings of pride,
    now that they have realized I'm living deep inside.
That night by their bedside they knelt in humble prayer,
    and thanked our Heavenly Father that I was living there.
They promised Him with all their might
    that they would raise me in the light.
And teach me all that I should know,
    of HIM, because they loved Him so.

When Mom went for her check-up, Doc set her heart a-whirl.
He listened with his stethoscope and said, "Sounds like a GIRL!
    I can tell by the rapid heartbeat . . ."
                       but what doctor doesn't know,
    it's just ME getting excited and too anxious to grow!

The weeks turned to months, it was ever so slow,
but each single day I could feel myself grow.
I thought about Earth in those long waiting hours,
I longed to see sunshine, I longed to smell flowers,
The adventure of a rainstorm that would splash in my face,
the beauty of a rainbow appearing in its place.

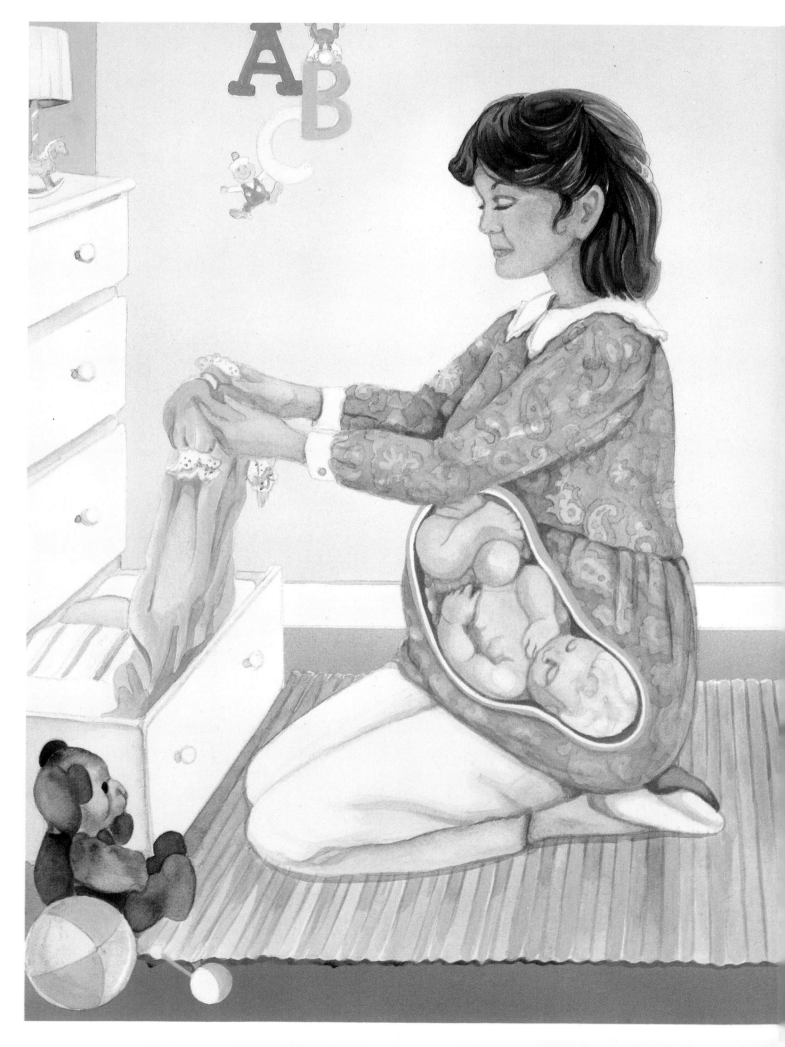

Then finally one day I felt so complete,
      my body was perfect, from my head to my feet.
For nine months now, Mom has cared for my needs,
      rocked me and fed me as she's gone about her deeds.
And though I've been content in this warm, cozy place;
      now I feel a longing to gaze upon her face.

I'm bored. I wonder what it's really like to be a child on EARTH?
I think this is going to be the morning of my birth!

So early on that Sunday morn, Mom felt a special glow;
she woke my father from his sleep and said, "It's TIME TO GO!"
Dad, trying to be calm, put on his car and drove his shoes . . .
directly to the hospital, with no time to lose!

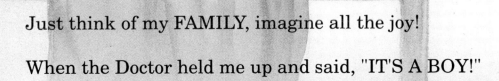

Just think of my FAMILY, imagine all the joy!

When the Doctor held me up and said, "IT'S A BOY!"

They wrapped me in a blanket,
    all snuggled soft and warm;
    then they gently laid me
    right in my Mother's arms.
And through her gentle tears,
    I could plainly see,
    that this was her, MY MOTHER,
      and she belonged to me!

"I've waited a lifetime to hold you,
    my precious little SON;
    and now our life together
    has finally just begun."

I yearned to tell them of the PLAN
    as Mother kissed my cheek;
    but when I tried, I only cried,
    I was too young to speak.

But I'll remember, Heavenly Father,
    I won't forget, you'll see.
As soon as I learn how to talk,
    I'll tell them about YOU and ME!